OPUS DEI

CHRISTIANS IN THE MIDST OF THE WORLD

by
Fr Peter Bristow

*All booklets are published thanks to the
generous support of the members of the
Catholic Truth Society*

CATHOLIC TRUTH SOCIETY
PUBLISHERS TO THE HOLY SEE

Contents

WHAT IS OPUS DEI?

In the spring of 2001, Pope John Paul II met a group of the faithful of Opus Dei from all over the world.[1] They included married couples with their young children, celibate men and women, priests, and the head of Opus Dei, Bishop Javier Echevarría. The Pope spoke to them at length about the role of the laity in the world.

'The Christian laity,' he pointed out, 'are charged with carrying out an apostolic mission. Their competence in various human activities is, in the first place, a God-given instrument "to enable the proclamation of Christ to reach peoples, mould communities, and have a deep and decisive influence in bringing Gospel values to bear in society and culture"[2]... Their apostolic zeal, fraternal friendship and loyal charity will enable them to turn daily social relationships into occasions to arouse in their colleagues that thirst for truth which is the first condition for the saving encounter with Christ.'[3]

This vision of lay men and women who put Christ into the heart of society through their ordinary work, acting as apostles to their friends and colleagues in daily life, is the same vision that moved a young Spanish priest, Fr Josemaría Escrivá, when God inspired him to found Opus Dei.

'St Paul gave a motto to the Christians at Ephesus,' said Fr Josemaría in one of his homilies, '*Instaurare omnia in Christo*: fill everything with the spirit of Jesus, placing Christ at the centre of everything... Our task as Christians is to proclaim this kingship of Christ, announcing it through what we say and do. Our Lord wants men and women of his own in all walks of life. Some he calls away from society, asking them to give up involvement in the world, so that they remind the rest of us by their example that God exists. To others he entrusts the priestly ministry. But he wants the vast majority to stay right where they are in all the earthly occupations in which they work: the factory, the laboratory, the farm, the trades, the streets of the big cities and the trails of the mountains.'[4] And in 1930, in a letter outlining the spirit of Opus Dei, he wrote: 'The ordinary, workaday, hidden life can be a way of holiness. It is not necessary to abandon your place in the world in order to seek God... for all the ways of the earth can present us with an opportunity to meet Christ.'

In this, as he pointed out, he was only going back to the Gospel, because Our Lord had exhorted *all* his followers in the Sermon on the Mount to 'be perfect, as your heavenly Father is perfect.'[5] In the words of Fr Josemaría, this message of Opus Dei is 'as old as the Gospel - and new as the Gospel is always new.'[6] But he was emphasising an aspect of the Gospel that had fallen into disuse. Although it was well known to the early Christians, over the centuries the idea that lay people were called to become saints slipped into the background.

So it was that Mgr Talbot, an English cleric working in Rome in the nineteenth century, was able to make his notoriously dismissive comment in reference to Cardinal Newman's promotion of the lay faithful: 'What is the province of the laity? To hunt, to shoot, to entertain.' To be 'laity' was something negative: a lay person was simply someone who was *not* a cleric, *not* a monk, *not* a nun. The laity were seen as passive units of a Church run exclusively by the clergy, rather than as responsible members of the faithful playing the part that corresponds to them in the Body of Christ. It took an Ecumenical Council, the Second Vatican Council, to remind the Church that 'all Christians, in any state or walk of life, are called to the fullness of Christian life and to the perfection of love.'[7]

When the Council Fathers talked in the Second Vatican Council about the full participation of the laity in the Church, they meant that lay people must take responsibility for the mission of the whole Church *in the world*: not simply in the liturgy and the parish, but in all walks of life and in all activities of human society. As John Paul II reminds us, the re-Christianisation of human affairs is imperative, the role of the laity is indispensable. This is especially true when it comes to the fields of the family, the workplace, culture and youth.

Many people have found a remarkable similarity between the teaching of the Second Vatican Council and many of

Opus Dei's ideas on the sanctification of the laity and on a renewed appreciation of the value of the world, especially a Christian's ordinary work and other activities. Up to the time of the Second Vatican Council, the world and its affairs tended to be seen as obstacles to Christian holiness, but for Fr Josemaría they were in fact, if used correctly, the meeting point with God. The vocation of lay people is to direct their human and everyday activity to God: this means that, far from being an impediment, this everyday activity becomes the very material of our holiness. The Second Vatican Council confirmed this vision when it taught that 'by reason of their special vocation, it belongs to the laity to seek the kingdom of God by engaging in the affairs of this world and directing them according to God's will.'[8]

Another document of the Council explains this further: 'The work of Christ's redemption concerns essentially the salvation of men; but it also takes in the renewal of the temporal order. The mission of the Church, consequently, is not only to bring men the message and grace of Christ, but also to permeate and improve the whole range of the temporal order. While carrying out this mission of the Church, the laity exercise their apostolate in the world as well as in the Church, in the temporal order as well as in the spiritual.'[9] Although the temporal and spiritual orders - the things of this world and the things of heaven - are distinct, they are closely linked in the divine plan, which is to contribute to the new creation that God will bring about at the end of time.

A Brief History

Josemaría Escrivá was born in Barbastro, a town in north-east Spain, in 1902, the second of six children. His father was a partner in a small textile business. He had a very ordinary childhood. When he had nearly reached his teens, however, the family underwent a series of misfortunes: Josemaría's three younger sisters died in consecutive years, and then his father's business went bankrupt, leaving them ruined. The family had to move to another town, Logroño, near the Basque country, and start again from scratch.

At the age of fifteen Josemaría was moved - by the sight of the bare footprints of a discalced Carmelite in the snow - to realise that God was asking something of him. He abandoned his plans of becoming an architect and entered the seminary. He was ordained in 1925. His father had died the previous year, leaving him head of the family. In 1927, with his bishop's permission, Fr Josemaría moved to Madrid with his family to work on his doctorate in law, something he had promised his father he would do.

During these years Fr Josemaría continued to search for the 'something' that God was asking of him. On 2nd October 1928, while he was doing a retreat in Madrid, God enabled him to *see* (as he later put it) Opus Dei. At first his foundation had no name and Fr Josemaría simply spoke about his 'work' or his 'apostolic work', until one day his confessor asked him: 'How is that "work of God" going?' Opus Dei means just that in Latin: 'Work of God.' Fr Josemaría saw this remark as providential: it provided a name for his 'work', and it was yet another indication that the initiative was not his but God's. God's initiative could be seen at other moments too: at first the founder thought that there would only be men in Opus Dei, and indeed he said so in writing - only to find shortly afterwards, while saying Mass on 14th February 1930, that Our Lord wanted it to be for women as well.

At this time the founder was working among the poor and the sick of Madrid as chaplain to a congregation of religious sisters. In addition to his chaplaincy duties, however, he was also carrying out an extensive pastoral work among all social groups, especially university students, from among whom came the first members of Opus Dei in the 1930s. His message to them was that holiness was not something for privileged people but for everybody, whatever their state in life and job or profession. Ordinary, everyday life can be a means of reaching holiness: it is not necessary to abandon one's place in the world, since all the paths of the earth can lead to an encounter with Christ.

This teaching was by no means common at the time - it would be another thirty years before the Second Vatican Council would speak of the 'universal call to sanctity.' As a result, there was neither a receptive environment for this message, nor the ascetical and spiritual doctrine. Neither was there a legal framework suitable for the new pastoral reality of Opus Dei. The Canon Law of the time had no place for an institution that incorporated both men and women and would also be able to have secular priests (not religious) in it. All this would take many years to bring about, and bears witness to the 'novelty' of Opus Dei. Because the mentality of the time was generally foreign to the idea of a calling to holiness and apostolate in the midst of the world, it did not appreciate the theological and ascetical richness of such a vocation. Fr Josemaría suffered many trials and tribulations as a result, and was branded a 'heretic' in some quarters for preaching it - despite the public support of the bishop of Madrid, who had given his encouragement to the founder from the start.

Not many years after the foundation he had to endure the religious persecution of the Spanish Civil War. Thousands of priests and religious were murdered in the Republican zone, and the clergy had to circulate incognito in order to avoid arrest and execution. At the beginning of the war a man who happened to look like Fr Josemaría was hanged - a case of mistaken identity, and one which moved Fr Josemaría to pray for that man's soul whenever he said Mass from then on. Despite the persecution he managed to continue exercising his priestly ministry, saying Mass when and where it was safe to do so and hearing confessions in the street. He even preached a retreat, moving with his retreatants from one safe house to another for the different activities.

After eighteen months of war Fr Josemaría decided to risk crossing over to the Nationalist zone, where the Church was able to operate freely. This meant taking a circuitous route via Barcelona and escaping over the mountains in the winter into Andorra. From there it was possible to go into France and then back into Spain further along the frontier. The journey of some ten days, walking mainly by night, was extremely rigorous, and his spiritual sons, the members of Opus Dei making the crossing with him, feared that in his undernourished state he might not survive it. Furthermore, it was dangerous: local smugglers frequently took these parties - sometimes numbering upwards of forty people - across the mountains, but the practice was known to the military authorities, who sent out patrols to intercept them. If an escape party was caught they were invariably all shot. This happened to a group shortly prior to Fr Josemaría's. He succeeded in crossing and returned to the Nationalist zone of Spain, where he found a place to stay in Burgos. From there he gave priestly attention to his followers and other young men he directed spiritually, many of whom were fighting at the front but would come to see him whenever they had a few days' leave.

As soon as the civil war was over Fr Josemaría returned to Madrid. Thanks to the zeal and dedication of the founder, Opus Dei grew rapidly from 1939 onwards and spread to various Spanish cities, though it was unable to go to any other countries during the Second World War. In 1941 it received its first formal written Church approval at diocesan level, from the bishop of Madrid. On 14th February 1943, after many years of prayer, Fr Josemaría finally came to see how there could be priests in Opus Dei, and founded the Priestly Society of the Holy Cross. The next year, 1944, the bishop of Madrid ordained the first three priests of Opus Dei. Among them was Alvaro del Portillo, who was to be the founder's successor.

Fr Josemaría moved to Rome in 1946 and governed Opus Dei from there until his death in 1975. In order to give his spiritual sons and daughters in Opus Dei the opportunity to receive a more intense formation in the spirit and specific apostolates of Opus Dei and do further studies in theology and other ecclesiastical subjects, he established in Rome the College of the Holy Cross for men and the College of Our Lady for women in 1948 and 1953 respectively.

On 24th February 1947, shortly after the founder's arrival in Rome, Opus Dei was approved as a world-wide institution of the Church. This was followed by a definitive pontifical approval dated 16th June 1950. Among other things, the new approval allowed for married people to join Opus Dei. It also allowed for diocesan priests to join the Priestly Society of the Holy Cross, so that they could benefit from the spiritual means offered by Opus Dei while remaining under their own bishop's jurisdiction. In 1982 Opus Dei became a personal prelature.

Opus Dei came to Britain at the end of 1946, and by the death of the founder in 1975 it was established in 32 countries. Since that time it has spread to a further 28 countries: apostolic work began in the former Eastern Bloc countries of Poland, Hungary and the Czech Republic in 1990, Nicaragua in 1992, India and Israel in 1993, Lithuania in 1994, Estonia, Slovakia, Lebanon and Uganda in 1996, the former Soviet republic of Kazakhstan in 1997 and South Africa in 1998. At the present the Opus Dei prelature is working in 60 countries and has some 84,000 faithful, most of whom are married, and around 1,750 priests who form the clergy of the prelature.

Fr Josemaría spent five summers in Great Britain, from 1958 to 1962. While here he took a special interest in St Thomas More, and visited his tomb in Canterbury. He saw in the great English saint a clear historical example of what it is to be an ordinary Christian who lives his faith fully, and he made him an intercessor of Opus Dei. The founder also greatly encouraged the apostolic work of the members of Opus Dei in Britain and was directly instrumental in the setting up of a centre of Opus Dei in Oxford in 1959, and a university residence in Manchester in 1960.

In the early 1950s he had already conceived the idea of setting up an international students' hall of residence in London. Today that hall of residence, Netherhall House, provides accommodation for over 100 students from about 30 countries. There is a homely atmosphere for the residents and freedom of religion is especially respected. An opportunity is provided for the residents to learn about Christianity through Catholic services and doctrinal talks, and Netherhall has had its share of converts to the Faith; but the spirit of Opus Dei has always been that these activities should be freely chosen and never obligatory in its centres. Some of the people who helped the work of Opus Dei to begin in countries such as Kenya, Nigeria, Hong Kong and Singapore first came into contact with Opus Dei in Netherhall House, bearing out Fr Josemaría's view of the importance of London as 'a crossroads of the world.'

After the founder's death, more than a third of the bishops of the world wrote to Pope Paul VI to ask him to start the cause of beatification and canonisation. The cause proceeded rapidly, thanks to a simplification of the procedures as a result of a desire expressed at the Second Vatican Council that Christians should be presented with more modern examples of holiness and figures in closer touch with contemporary life. The consultors of the Congregation for Saints saw in the founder of Opus Dei both a figure who provided a spirituality for lay people, fully rooted in their secular character, and also someone sent by God to reawaken the Church to the needs of re-evangelisation. Fr Josemaría was beatified by Pope John Paul II on 17th May 1992, just seventeen years after his death, in the presence of about 300,000 people including 33 cardinals and over 200 bishops from all over the world.

Blessed Josemaría Escrivá (centre) with his two successors in turn, Alvaro del Portillo (left) and Javier Echevarría (right) outside St Dunstan's Church, Canterbury (1958).

THE MESSAGE OF OPUS DEI

The message of Opus Dei has its roots in the vocation and commitment that the Christian receives at baptism. By baptism a Christian is incorporated into Christ and becomes an active member of the People of God, namely the Church. As a result, each member of the Church (whether they are lay people, or religious, or priests or bishops) is called to holiness and apostolate, because they have been given a share in the divine life, which is destined to lead to eternal life. Holiness, then, means union with God and the attainment of the blessedness to which we are all destined. It is achieved by developing all the virtues, following the path of the beatitudes which Our Lord marked out. Fr Josemaría often referred to St Paul's words to the Ephesians, addressed to all Christians: God 'chose us... before the foundation of the world that we should be holy and blameless before him.'[10]

The first reaction of the average lay person to the idea that they are called to holiness - that is, to become saints - is often to say something like, 'What, me, a saint? You must be joking.' Yet on further investigation you usually find that the same people confidently hope and expect to get to heaven. They haven't reflected sufficiently on the fact that holiness and getting to heaven are the same thing. Fr Josemaría emphasised that there is no such thing as 'second-class' holiness: everybody, whatever their state in life, is called to live fully in accordance with their faith and seek the perfection of love.

The message of lay holiness, however, will always need explanation, exhortation and repetition. Take the following story. A teacher at a Catholic school was just about to begin a class one day when a pupil asked: 'Please, sir, why do we have a crucifix in the classroom?' Caught unawares by the question, the teacher answered, 'I suppose it's to show that what we are going to do now isn't really important.' This attitude comes about because we tend to separate religion from everyday life, so the Gospel is made to seem remote from daily activities. Fr Josemaría used to say that 'our human vocation is an important part of our divine vocation',[11] and they should not be unduly separated.

Finding God in ordinary things

We tend to act as if the important things in life - God, holiness, our growth in virtue, sinfulness and our attitude to the suffering of others - can be settled later. Though deep down we know they *should* make an impact on our everyday lives, we tend to be puzzled as to how these things can be linked to passing exams, earning a living, making a success of our job, getting the car or the washing machine mended, paying the mortgage and so on. What this means is that we fail to see the link between our lives as working people, family people, and our Christian vocation.

Fr Josemaría was unequivocal in his insistence that we must find God in and through these things. He warned against the danger of leading a kind of double life: 'On the one side, an interior life, a life of relation with God; and on the other, a separate and distinct working, social and family life, full of small earthly realities. No!' he exclaimed in a striking phrase, 'we cannot have a split personality if we want to be Christians.'[12] There should be a coherence between being a Christian and acting like one in all circumstances, a coherence he described as 'unity of life.' 'We discover the invisible God in the most visible and material things... Either we learn to find Our Lord in ordinary, everyday life, or we shall never find him.'[13] If sanctity is for everybody then it must be found in the ordinary mundane things of each day because the majority of people do not have the opportunity to do extraordinary things most of the time. For an ordinary Christian, corresponding to the grace of God consists principally in striving to fulfil perfectly the duties of his or her state in life.

Many perhaps miss the fullness of the Christian vocation because they do not see that it applies to the small and apparently insignificant details of ordinary life, such as a gesture of friendship and affection or the writing of a letter or payment of a bill, or the decoration of the house. The idea that great sanctity can be achieved in the faithful fulfilment of the little and ordinary duties of each day is a common doctrine of the Church, advocated by saints and ecclesiastical writers through the centuries. The founder of Opus Dei preached it with uncommon emphasis: 'Your ordinary contact with God takes place where your fellow men, your yearnings, your work and your affections are. There you have your daily encounter with Christ... It leads you to do your work perfectly by putting love in the little things of everyday life, and discovering that divine something which is hidden in small details. The lines of a Castilian poet are especially appropriate here: "Write slowly and with a careful hand, for doing things well is more important than doing them"... That is why I have told you repeatedly, and hammered away once and again on the idea, that the Christian vocation consists in making heroic verse out of the prose of each day. Heaven and earth seem to merge, my children, on the horizon. But where they really meet is in your hearts, when you sanctify your everyday lives.'[14]

Fr Josemaría used to say that the easiest way to understand Opus Dei is to think of the early Christians. They lived as equals among their fellow citizens, yet at the same time there were obvious differences. As an early Christian document, the *Letter to Diognetus*, puts it, Christians 'are to the world what the soul is to the body. They live in the world but are not worldly, as the soul is in the body but is not corporeal. They live in every town and city, as the soul is in every part of the body. They work from within and pass unnoticed, as the soul does of its essence... They live

as pilgrims among perishable things with their eyes set on
the immortality of heaven, as the immortal soul dwells
now in a perishable house. Their numbers increase daily
amid persecutions, as the soul is made beautiful amid
mortifications... And Christians have no right to abandon
their mission in the world, in the same way as the soul
may not voluntarily separate itself from the body.'[15]

Sanctifying work and renewing the world

Most men and women are called to imitate the hidden
life of Our Lord and they do this in their work and in
living their family life. Again, the Second Vatican
Council points out that lay people 'are called by God so
that, being led by the spirit of the Gospel, they may contribute to the sanctification of the world as from within,
like leaven, by fulfilling their own particular duties... It
pertains to them [the laity] to illuminate and order all
temporal things... to Christ.' [16] This is done when they
endeavour to imitate Christ, whose contemporaries
remarked that he 'did all things well.'[17] Christ's life has
returned work to its true purpose, which is to co-operate
in God's work of creation. And Christ has also made
work, for Christians, a way of sanctification and co-
redemption. For members of Opus Dei, Fr Josemaría
emphasised, work is the 'hinge of their sanctification.'[18]

The members of Opus Dei do not simply strive to sanctify themselves through their work, but also to sanctify the

work itself, and to sanctify others with their work. 'The characteristic of the lay state being a life led in the midst of the world and of secular affairs, lay people are called by God to make of their apostolate... a leaven in the world.'[19] But united as they are to the Mystical Body, their work also becomes part of the apostolate of the Church when through it they renew the world in the spirit of Christ and further the message of evangelisation and salvation.

Carried out under these conditions all honest work, whether domestic or manual chores, professional or business activity, or creative or artistic labour, can and should be a way to God. What God asks of us is to put our particular talents to good use. 'Go and trade with them until I come back,' he tells us in the parable.[20] 'Lay people ought to take on themselves as their distinctive task this renewal of the temporal order.'[21] What do we mean by the 'temporal order'? The Second Vatican Council answers: 'personal and family values, culture, economic interests, the trades and professions, institutions of the political community, international relations and so on.'[22] 'The lay faithful... can be active in this particular moment of history in areas of culture, in the arts and theatre, scientific research, labour, means of communication, politics and the economy...'[23]

Work is normally done for noble human motives, such as earning a living for our family, using our talents, and contributing to the progress of society. And precisely because these are genuine human values, human work can be raised to the divine level. Fr Josemaría put it this way: 'Nothing can be foreign to Christ's care. If we enter into the theology of it... we cannot say that there are things - good, noble or indifferent - which are exclusively worldly. This cannot be after the Word of God has lived among the children of men, felt hunger and thirst, worked with his hands, experienced friendship and obedience and suffering and death. "For in him all the fullness of God was pleased to dwell, and through him to reconcile to himself all things, whether on earth or in heaven, making peace by the blood of his cross."[24] We must love the world and work and all human things. For the world is good. Adam's sin destroyed the divine balance of creation; but God the Father sent his only Son to re-establish peace, so that we, his children by adoption, might free creation from disorder and reconcile all things to God.'[25]

Sanctifying our work means, in the first place, working in accordance with the laws of the country and general moral norms; but it also means working with a desire to serve our fellow citizens and contribute to the progress of society. And it means that we are constantly searching for union with God while we are doing it. As Fr Josemaría wrote in one of his books of spirituality, 'an hour of study, for a modern apostle, is an hour of prayer',[26] and he taught members of Opus Dei that to achieve their purpose they had to strive to become 'contemplatives in the midst of the world.'[27]

Sanctifying work also presupposes the fundamental goodness of the world that God created and sees work as a co-operation with that. It is true the world is defaced by man's sins, but Scripture teaches also that man was *created* in order to work, even before original sin occurred.[28] By his Incarnation and his hidden life - years of ordinary physical labour at the carpenter's bench - Christ has made work into 'something both redeemed and redeeming',[29] and thus given back to it the dimension it had before the Fall, that of praising God and co-operating with Him. And since the whole of Our Lord's life, from the moment of the Incarnation onwards, is redemptive, for a Christian work becomes a participation in both the creation and the redemption.

There can, of course, be a wrong attitude to work and human activity, as when it is done for purely material gain and greed, or out of vanity and egoism. That is why it is vital to strive to be 'a contemplative in the midst of the world' and to do one's work for the glory of God and the service of others. Pope John Paul II made this point at the founder's beatification: 'In a society in which an unbridled craving for material things turns them into idols and a cause of separation from God, the new Blessed reminds us that the same realities, creatures of God and of human industry, if correctly used for the glory of the Creator and the service of one's brothers and sisters, can be a way for men and women to meet Christ. "All things of the earth," he taught, "including the earthly and temporal activity of men and women, must be directed to God"... The relevance and transcendence of this spiritual message, deeply rooted in the Gospel, are evident, as is also shown in the fruitfulness with which God has blessed the life and work of Josemaría Escrivá.'[30]

Fr Josemaría's message emphasises the full, positive and indeed irreplaceable vocation of the lay Christian to sanctity and apostolate. Men and women have the role of proclaiming the kingdom of Christ through their work and family life. In this way they are contributing to the sanctification and renewal of the world from within. This positive outlook goes beyond a way of thinking that has grown up which sees the Christian faith in terms of dos and don'ts, or of going to Mass on Sunday and then ignoring God for all practical purposes for the rest of the week; of treating our religious duties as somehow an appendage to the rest of our lives, rather than as an integral part of them. The baptismal vocation covers everything in our lives and we have to contribute to making all the paths of the earth divine.

Family life

The teaching of the Second Vatican Council sees the Church as a Body, in which each member of the baptised has his or her part to play in building up the whole Body, and highlights the areas of family life and work. It says of parents and spouses that 'they stand as witnesses and co-operators of the fruitfulness of mother Church, as a sign of and a share in that love with which Christ loved his bride and gave himself for her.'[31]

In imitation of the Holy Family, the Christian family has to be the 'domestic Church', that is a school of love and virtue, piety and doctrine and a place where the families of the future are nurtured. The spirit of Opus Dei leads its members to imitate particularly the hidden life of Our Lord and hence the shining example of his family life in Nazareth. The formation given to married members of Opus Dei aims to help spouses live out the truth that marriage is a sign and instrument of God's love for the Church and for men and women.

Fr Josemaría wrote, 'The purpose of marriage is to help married people sanctify themselves and others. For this reason they receive a special grace in the sacrament instituted by Jesus Christ. Those who are called to the married state will, with the grace of God, find within their state everything they need to be holy, to identify themselves each day more with Jesus Christ, and to lead those with whom they live to God... the secret of married happiness lies in everyday things, not in daydreams. It lies in finding the hidden joy of coming home in the evening; in everyday work in which the whole family co-operates; in good humour in the face of difficulties that should be met with a sporting spirit; in making the best use of all the advances that civilisation offers to help us bring up children, to make the house pleasant and life more simple.'[32]

Apostolate and evangelisation

The *Catechism of the Catholic Church* states that 'the faithful exercise their baptismal priesthood through their participation, each according to his own vocation, in Christ's mission as priest, prophet and king.'[33] Priests, by their ordination, share in the *ministerial* priesthood of Christ with the task and the power of representing Christ as Head of the Church, announcing the Word of God and celebrating the sacraments. But lay people share in the *common* priesthood of Christ as a result of their baptism, and they too have a task and a power that comes from their own specific share in the priesthood of Christ.[34] It is through them that the Church will reach the de-Christianised and un-churched masses of modern life. It is not enough simply to wait for men and women to come to church on their own initiative: many will not. What is needed is for all the baptised to act as a leaven which raises the spiritual temperature of society and brings the Gospel to the world. Their task is to spread the faith in their family, in their work, in their social activities and in all the circumstances and events of their life. Fr Josemaría expressed this point by saying that the members of Opus Dei should have a priestly soul and lay outlook.

In his letter *Christ's Lay Faithful*, the Pope likens the laity to the labourers in the parable sent into the vineyard of the world.[35] The laity's task, therefore, is to build up the Body of Christ in the world, and the lay Christian needs no other authorisation or commitment to do this than the grace of Baptism. The apostolate of members of Opus Dei is based on their friendship and trust with those around them, so normally it is done on a personal and one-to-one basis and not collectively. They strive to be more fully aware of Our Lord's words, 'if salt has lost its taste how shall its saltiness be restored?... Neither do men light a lamp and put it under a bushel, but on a lampstand, to give light to all in the house.'[36]

The Opus Dei prelature forms its members to play their part in this task with their personal apostolate, and through the apostolic initiatives they promote in collaboration with others. These apostolic initiatives include schools and universities, youth clubs and homework centres for young people, hospitals and agricultural schools.

However, together with a priestly soul, Fr Josemaría spoke of having a lay outlook. It is worthwhile pondering more on what he meant by this term. We should not overlook the fact that the things of the world have their own proper autonomy under God, and this fact will influence the ordinary lay Christian's way of doing apostolate. Fr Josemaría said in a homily in 1967, 'A man who knows that the world, and not just the church, is the place where he finds Christ, loves that world. He endeavours to become properly trained, intellectually and professionally. He makes up his own mind with complete freedom about the problems of the environment in which he moves, and he takes his own decisions in consequence. As the decisions of a Christian, they derive from personal reflection, which endeavours in all humility to grasp the will of God in both the unimportant and the important events of his life.'[37] A Catholic with this kind of lay perspective does not think that he represents the Church to the world, or that he can give '*the* Catholic solution' to the problems of the world. Having a lay outlook leads Christians to take personal responsibility for their own actions and decisions, to respect the freedom of others in temporal matters, and not to make use of the Church for their own ends or involve her in human factions.

The message of Opus Dei is a reminder to the laity that the fullness of Christian life belongs also to them. The world God created is good, though it has been defiled by sin, and it is the Christian's task to play his or her part in renewing it in the spirit of Christ: all things have to be restored in Christ, and it is the task of Christians throughout time to contribute to that process. It is particularly urgent at the present time. Pope John Paul II has repeatedly expressed the need for society to be re-Christianised. Such an enormous enterprise can only be carried out by the faithful as a whole, priests, religious and lay people, each playing their part to the full.

While saying Mass on the feast of the Transfiguration in 1931, Fr Josemaría was reminded interiorly and with great force of some words of Our Lord in the Gospel, 'If I am lifted up from the earth I will draw all things to myself.'[38] 'I understood,' he wrote immediately afterwards, 'that it would be the men and women of God who would lift up the Cross with the teachings of Christ, placing it at the summit of all human activity. And I saw Our Lord triumph and draw all things to himself.'

'A secret, an open secret,' Fr Josemaría wrote in *The Way*: 'these world crises are crises of saints. God wants a handful of men "of his own" in every human activity. And then... *pax Christi in regno Christi* - the peace of Christ in the kingdom of Christ.'[39] And again, 'Don't you long to shout to those young men and women all around you: Fools, leave those worldly things that shackle the heart and very often degrade it... leave all that and come with us in search of love!'[40]

VOCATION AND SPIRIT

To join Opus Dei you need a vocation. This is a specific personal calling within the general calling to holiness which each person receives at baptism. As with any other vocation there is an interior change, a commitment to serve God with your whole life according to the spirit of Opus Dei, but externally your life normally continues with relatively little change. The call to Opus Dei does not take anyone out of their place or state in life. 'What amazes you seems natural to me: that God should have chosen you out in the exercise of your profession! That is how he sought the first, Peter and Andrew, James and John, beside their nets, and Matthew sitting in the customhouse. And - wonder of wonders! - Paul, in his eagerness to destroy the seed of the Christians.'[41] This is how it works in Opus Dei.

A vocation involves an interior conversion, a profound awareness of the commitment to fulfil your baptismal promises, living all the consequences of being a Christian, directing all things to God and serving him in your interior dispositions and external actions. A generous response to the divine call means shaping your life around it, in the classic manner of the prophet Samuel: 'Here I am, Lord, because you called me.'[42] It involves making yourself available to carry out God's plans, determined to eliminate from your life anything that is incompatible with them. This is borne out in St Luke's Gospel by the parable of the King (representing God) who becomes angry with the invited guests who refuse the invitation to the royal banquet (an image of the kingdom of Heaven), even though they seemed to have valid professional and family reasons not to attend.[43]

This all-embracing nature of God's call and the requirement to put the kingdom of God first are brought out on other occasions in the Gospels. The rich young man, after asserting that he has fulfilled the Commandments, is asked to give up everything to follow Our Lord - that is, to surrender both himself and his belongings in order to be totally available to God. Our Lord goes on to promise those who follow him, giving up family ties and future human possibilities, a hundredfold reward as well as eternal life.[44] The man who wants to bury his father before beginning to proclaim the Good News is told, 'Let the dead bury the dead',[45] and the one who wants to bid farewell to his family is told that 'no-one who puts his hand to the plough and looks back is fit for the kingdom of Heaven.'[46]

Christ is laying down the order of priorities our lives should have, and perhaps on some occasions he insists on immediate fulfilment because he knows that, if the people concerned delay their response, they are in danger of losing the grace of vocation altogether. Naturally, he expects us to love our families - but according to an order which puts God first. Since we are supposed to love others in Christ there should be no opposition between the love we owe to

God and that which we owe to our neighbour, be it parent, brother, sister, spouse or friend. Fr Josemaría liked to refer to the Fourth Commandment to love father and mother as the 'sweet Commandment', and he said of the members of Opus Dei that they owed ninety per cent of their vocation to their parents.[47] Experience shows that those who follow their vocation with supernatural faith and generosity - which is the vast majority - love their families more than before, even though they may perhaps see them less.

The vocation to Opus Dei is the same for all members. Although people join as supernumeraries, numeraries, or associates, these do not represent grades or categories of membership but rather three ways of living one and the same vocation, with the same spirit and the same degree of commitment, depending on one's particular circumstances and state of life. Supernumeraries make up by far the largest part of Opus Dei, accounting at present for 70% of its faithful. They are usually married men and women whose principal calling is to sanctify their work and their family duties. Numeraries live celibacy, and so are fully available to attend to the needs of the prelature and help in the spiritual formation of the others, while at the same time making this compatible with the tasks of their ordinary working day. They ordinarily live in centres of the prelature (men and women separately). Associates are also celibate; but family responsibilities or personal circumstances make them less available for the apostolates of the prelature and they normally live with their own families, or wherever is most suited to their work and other circumstances.

Most numeraries have ordinary jobs, but their home is an Opus Dei centre where they live with other numeraries; and it is in the centres that the cheerful and affectionate family atmosphere which is part of the spirit of Opus Dei is particularly visible. The bonds of the residents of a centre with one another find expression in attending some spiritual activities - especially Holy Mass - together, as well as in prayer and sacrifice for one another; but it can be seen more obviously in the care, concern and mutual affection that should be present in any Christian family. Residents will make an effort to return to the centre every day for dinner and a get-together in the evening, in order to spend some time with one another. They will celebrate birthdays and special anniversaries just as in any normal family. Fr Josemaría often gathered the first members of Opus Dei at his mother's house for meetings and family get-togethers and his mother and sister generously helped to look after the domestic administration of the first Opus Dei centres, thus initiating the family spirit of warmth, mutual affection and cheerfulness that is typical of the centres today.

A lay spirit

The spirit of Opus Dei is perfectly suited to the condition of being a lay person, as it is deeply rooted in the fact of our being children of God - the consecration of our baptism

- and our common task of bringing the world to Christ. Because little attention was given to the laity or their spirituality in past centuries, they often had to make do with a spirituality adapted from that of the religious orders. The world was commonly seen as a place of dangers, work as a distraction from the true purpose of life. By insisting on the sanctification of work and the family and the fullness of the Christian vocation lived in the world and by evoking the lives of the first Christians, who lived as equals among their contemporaries but without sharing their pagan and immoral customs, Fr Josemaría established not just a new spirituality but a new *type* of spirituality. As Cardinal Luciani wrote a month before he became Pope John Paul I, he 'did not just produce a spirituality for lay people, but he developed a genuinely lay spirituality.'[48]

The spirit of Opus Dei can be found both in the published works and the as-yet unpublished documents and letters that the founder wrote for his spiritual children. His published works include books of spiritual considerations, *The Way, Furrow* and *The Forge*, as well as collections of homilies, *Christ is Passing By, Friends of God* and *In Love with the Church*, and *Conversations with Monsignor Escrivá*, a collection of interviews with journalists.

Forming the laity

The activity of Opus Dei can be summed up by saying that it consists in forming the faithful of the prelature so that they can carry out a wide range of apostolic activities, in their own place in the Church and the world, in their families and at work and in their social relations. In this way they support the evangelising work of the pastors of the Church and proclaim the universal call to holiness to those around them. Fr Josemaría was convinced that the poor practice of Christian life in so many places was due in large measure to the fact that people were ignorant of the truth Christ came to bring. It was therefore necessary for the faithful of Opus Dei to study and learn Christian doctrine and in turn teach it to others. In the words of the founder, Opus Dei is a 'great catechesis.'

For lay people to become saints and to carry out apostolic work, they need to be formed in spiritual, doctrinal and personal areas. This is all the more necessary since not all of what passes for education is really formative, in the sense that it enables us to exercise our freedom in accordance with the truth: we need to learn how to live the virtues in their fullness in a secular context.

For example, the virtue of poverty as preached in the Sermon on the Mount is something required of all the followers of Christ. Lay people may think of poverty in the monastic sense of materially giving up everything: then, when they find they cannot do this, they begin to believe it is not for them. John Paul II, however, says that Jesus' words to the rich young man apply to everyone.[49] In fact, the Christian virtue of poverty means everyone can possess whatever they require in order to fulfil the duties of their state in life; but they should aim not to have more than they need, and to use the things they have as means and not ends in themselves. Lay people, in fact, have to live real poverty as something tangible, without at the same time following unrealistic, preconceived rules. They do this by learning how to do without the superfluous, and sometimes making sacrifices to do without what is necessary in order to give generously to good and needy causes. Fr Josemaría suggested as a general criterion that each one consider himself to be a father or mother of a large and poor family when making decisions of this type. All the virtues have to be learnt and re-learnt, as Isaiah reminded us with the words, 'Learn to do good.'[50] With poverty as with all the other virtues, it is a matter of being *in* the world but not *of* it, being secular but not worldly.

What is needed in the first place to nourish our own spiritual lives is knowledge of the faith - that is, of the Scriptures, the life of Christ and the teaching of the Church. St Jerome says, 'Ignorance of the Scriptures is ignorance of Christ.' To this end, members of Opus Dei spend some time each day reading from the New Testament and from a spiritual book, so as to provide themselves increasingly with food for meditation. Study of doctrine, however, is also required for the needs of evangelisation and in order to provide a Christian response to all the issues which modern life and the media continue to throw up - questions of family morality, medical ethics, social justice, ecumenism, the environment and so on. All of this forms part of the strengthening of our own faith as well as the proclamation of Christian and human truth in different walks of life.

A trained Christian will have the confidence to demonstrate that the Church's mission is indeed to serve the world with the truth, and particularly the family and the world of work. Newman spoke in the same vein some hundred and fifty years ago, in his lectures on the position of Catholics in England at the time: 'What I desire in Catholics is the gift of bringing out what their religion is; it is one of those "better gifts", of which the Apostle bids you be "zealous". You must not hide your talent in a napkin, or your light under a bushel.' This training is made available to all the faithful of Opus Dei, who are given the opportunity to study the faith to the extent to which they are able, depending on their capacities and the time they have available.

High on the agenda of Christian formation for Fr Josemaría was learning to respect the dignity of man and one of its consequences, individual freedom. He wrote, 'The Christian should defend all the rights which the dignity of man confers upon him. There is one right in particular which one should always seek: personal freedom.'[51] To respect and love the dignity of each individual goes to the heart of charity, which is why he often said, 'More than in giving, charity consists in understanding.'[52]

He wrote that respect for freedom stems from love. 'If others do not look at things the same way as I do, can this be a reason for considering them my enemies? Such an attitude can only be motivated by the selfishness and intellectual short-sightedness of one who feels there are no other values beyond those of politics and temporal affairs. For the Christian, however, it is not so, because each person is of infinite value and has an eternal destiny in God: Christ died for each one of us.'[53]

Children of God

The basis of the spirit of Opus Dei is the awareness of being a son or daughter of God. St Peter said that Christians were 'partakers of the divine nature',[54] because as a result of the Redemption, man is invited to share God's own life. It is this which makes us one with God, members of Christ and of his family, the Church, and able to live in ever-closer communion with him. Man's creation in the 'image and likeness of God' had already given him the capability of sharing the divine life. After the Redemption he can be - and is expected to become - 'another Christ', indeed 'Christ himself.' Fr Josemaría used a favourite word of the Greek Fathers for this process, divinisation: 'Our faith teaches us that man in the state of grace, is divinised - filled with God... And this *divinisation* affects everything human; it is a sort of foretaste of the final resurrection.'[55]

Recognising that we are children of God has to be more than something theoretical: it should have direct consequences in our daily lives. The founder of Opus Dei wrote, 'We must try to be children who realise that the Lord, by loving us as his children, has taken us into his house, in the midst of the world, to be members of his family so that what is his is ours, and what is ours is his; and to develop that familiarity and confidence which prompts us to ask him, like children, for the moon.'[56] It enables us to see the loving hand of God in the ordinary events of each day and to act at the same time as children of God and as responsible citizens who carry out our family, work-related and social duties. An immediate consequence, then, of realising that we are children of God is a unity of life, a coherence between our spiritual and material duties, that leads us to live our faith with integrity and to be able to stand up for our rights because we fulfil our duties.

The everyday existence of work and family life, therefore, are the ordinary setting for accomplishing the divinisation that should come from being children of God in fulfilment of our Christian vocation. The practice of remembering in our daily lives that we are children of God gives joy to those who follow it because, as St Paul says, 'all things work out for the good of those who love God',[57] and because Christ came that we might share in his joy and peace.[58]

Daily conversion and interior struggle

Fr Josemaría taught that holiness is not just for 'perfect' people but for ordinary people, and hence for sinners - as long as they are ready to be converted and begin anew each day in the struggle to love God above all things. This involves an interplay between God's grace and human response, so the sacraments are crucial in providing daily nourishment and strength for the soul. As sin is the true evil that separates us from sanctity, Fr Josemaría repeatedly emphasised the need for frequent recourse to the sacrament of penance. This is the way in which the infinite mercy of God is conveyed and is the path to conversion of life and renewal of soul. In *The Way*, he wrote, 'What depths of mercy there are in God's justice! For, in the judgements of men, he who confesses his fault is punished: and in the judgement of God he is pardoned. Blessed be the holy sacrament of penance!' And he added, '"Put on the Lord Jesus Christ," says St Paul to the Romans. It is in the sacrament of penance that you and I put on Jesus Christ and his merits.'[59]

And to know and do God's will fully, he advised spiritual direction with a priest who can get to know us well and is thus able to offer sound guidance. 'Conversion is the task of a moment; sanctification is the work of a lifetime... Therefore, we must be ready to begin again, to find again - in new situations - the light and the stimulus of our first conversion.'[60]

'In this adventure of love,' Fr Josemaría said, 'we should not be depressed by our falls, not even by serious falls if we go to God in the sacrament of penance contrite and resolved to improve. A Christian is not a neurotic collector of good behaviour reports. Jesus Christ, Our Lord, was moved as much by Peter's repentance after his fall as by John's innocence and faithfulness. Jesus understands our weakness and draws us to himself up a gentle slope. He wants us to make an effort to climb a little each day. He seeks us out, just as he did the disciples of Emmaus, whom he went out to meet. He sought Thomas, showed himself to him and made him touch with his fingers the open wounds in his hands and his side. Jesus Christ is waiting for us to return to him; he knows our weakness.'[61]

On a practical level, Fr Josemaría used to advise people to adopt a cheerful, 'sporting spirit' in the face of the events of the day, not being depressed by their failures in their interior struggle but simply picking themselves up with a smile, and trying to do better next time round. And in a get-together after the 1972 Olympics he cited - and acted out, to the great amusement of his listeners - the example of the pole-vaulter who, having failed to clear the bar first time, gets up and tries again until he succeeds.

Prayer and interior life

The founder of Opus Dei stressed that in order to sanctify our daily activity two conditions above all are necessary:

prayer and sacrifice. 'First prayer, then atonement, in the
third place, very much in the third place, action', he wrote
in *The Way*.[62] He would say, unless you teach young people
to have interior life and do mental prayer you have wasted
your time. On more than one occasion he surprised married
men and women by telling them they had to be 'contemplatives in the midst of the world.' To be effective, your
active and apostolic life have to be the overflow of the
life within, he taught.

In emphasising that prayer is indispensable, Fr
Josemaría underlined the fact that holiness consists in
getting to know and love Christ and identifying ourselves
with him. But how can you get to love somebody you
don't know? And how can you know somebody you don't
talk to? He gave this advice, 'To follow Christ - that is the
secret. We must accompany him so closely that we come
to live with him, like the first twelve did; so closely that
we become identified with him. Soon we will be able to
say, provided we haven't put obstacles in the way of
grace, that we have put on, have clothed ourselves, with
Our Lord Jesus Christ.'[63] For many people he brought
alive the Gospel scenes and taught them how to meditate
on them and apply them to their daily lives. Nobody can
plead that they cannot pray, he taught, it is open to everybody: for prayer is simply talking with God and becoming
friends of Christ. It is not something that requires separation from daily activities; on the contrary, it has to be

woven into them. 'If you think you are not quite ready to pray, go to Jesus as his disciples did and say to him, 'Lord, teach us how to pray.' You will discover how the Holy Spirit "comes to the aid of our weakness"...'[64]

He also emphasised the importance of praying regularly each day, if possible at a fixed time, and not simply when one feels like it; in other words, a daily plan of life. The daily plan of life the members of Opus Dei follow includes a time for mental prayer, Holy Mass (which Fr Josemaría called 'the centre and root of the interior life'[65]), a visit to the Blessed Sacrament and an examination of conscience. This has the flexibility to fit in with a day's work and activities, he explained, in the way that a surgeon's glove covers the hand yet enables him to move his fingers freely.

The little cross of each day

The founder of Opus Dei made it clear that he was not proposing an easy route to holiness. It was a route that was accessible to all, but it required total self-giving and commitment - and the taking up of our daily cross.[66] This daily cross can sometimes be something very small: he gave the example, taken from an Irish spiritual writer, of someone who gave up butter on his toast for breakfast: 'We were reading - you and I - the heroically ordinary life of that man of God. And we saw him fight whole months and years (what "accounts" he kept in his particular examina-tion!) at breakfast time: today he won, tomorrow he was beaten... He noted: "Didn't have butter... did have butter!"' And he added, 'May you and I too live our "butter drama".'[67]

The cross of each day is found in the loving acceptance and fulfilment of the will of God, which normally comes in the ordinary events of every day and in the obligations we have taken on in our family, work and social lives. In Fr Josemaría's words (from the 1930 letter quoted earlier), 'There is no sanctity without the cross, without mortification. And we will find mortification most easily in ordinary, everyday matters - our orderly, unstinting, hard work. We must know that the best spirit of sacrifice is shown in perseverance; in finishing well the work we have begun; in being punctual and filling the day with 'heroic minutes'; in our care for the material things we have and use; in our zeal to serve, which makes us fulfil with care our smallest duties; and in our little acts of charity which make the path of sanctity in the world pleasant for everyone. At times a smile can be the greatest manifestation of our spirit of penance. On the other hand... it is not the true spirit of penance to make great sacrifices one day, and completely abandon mortification the next. You will have the spirit of penance when you know how to conquer yourself every day without any spectacular show, offering the Lord a thousand little things.'

This spirit of self-sacrifice, constant but in small things, can be compared to the self-discipline in training that every

sportsman or woman needs - an example that St Paul uses
when speaking of the Christian's self-sacrifice: 'Every ath-
lete must keep his appetites under control; and he does it to
win a wreath that fades, whereas ours is imperishable... I
buffet my body, and make it my slave; or I, who have
preached to others, might myself be disqualified.'[68] The
Christian difference, St Paul points out, is that rather than
sacrificing ourselves for our own personal ends - the ath-
lete's sporting success, the dieter's improved looks, the
overtime worker's promotion or bigger pay packet - we
sacrifice ourselves to imitate Christ and to share in his life.

It is in this spirit of imitating Christ that some members of Opus Dei also respond to Christ's invitation to
take up his cross by using traditional Christian practices
of self-denial including, in some cases, the use of corporal
mortification. These ascetical practices are no more harm-
ful than the jogging or dieting which many take up in
order to improve their health or their appearance. But
they are a means of sharing voluntarily, in a small way,
in the suffering of Jesus Christ, as many saints through
the centuries have done.

Devotion to Our Lady

The intimate role of Our Lady in the redemptive work of
her Son began at the time of the Incarnation and continued not only throughout her life but also after her earthly
existence. 'Taken up to heaven,' The Second Vatican

Council teaches, 'she did not lay aside this saving office but by her manifold intercession continues to bring us the gifts of eternal salvation. By her maternal charity, she cares for the brethren of her Son, who still journey on earth surrounded by dangers and difficulties, until they are led into their blessed home.'[69]

Even before founding Opus Dei, Fr Josemaría already practised the tender and solid piety of a son towards his heavenly Mother, based on the teachings of the faith and expressed in the time-honoured devotions. 'We go to Jesus and we return to him through Mary,'[70] he said. To foster this devotion to Our Lady, he encouraged his spiritual sons and daughters in Opus Dei to practise many of the Marian devotions established by the Church such as the Rosary and the Angelus, so that they would benefit from the maternal mediation of Mary and meditate frequently on her example of holiness: 'If we truly got to know Mary our Mother,' he wrote, 'how quickly the supernatural virtues would grow in us.'[71] He was very conscious that he could not have achieved all that he did in starting Opus Dei if it had not been for the powerful intercession of his Mother in Heaven.

His great devotion to Mary gave him a great love for the Holy Family, whom tradition calls the 'trinity on earth.' He sometimes said that he would like each Opus Dei centre to be 'a corner of the home at Nazareth.' This love could be seen also in his veneration for St Joseph, whom he made a patron saint of Opus Dei.

Love for the Church and the Pope

Fr Josemaría first arrived in Rome in 1946, after a journey from Spain by land and sea that lasted over twenty-four hours without the possibility of stopping to rest. Despite his exhaustion (aggravated by the serious diabetes from which he was suffering), he spent the whole of his first night on the balcony of his flat within sight of the Vatican, praying for the Pope. His love and veneration for the Pope led him frequently to request prayers for the Holy Father, and he wrote (in 1934), 'Christ, Mary, the Pope. Have we not indicated in these three words the loves which sum up our entire Catholic faith?'

Fr Josemaría made his own St Cyprian's remark that 'nobody can have God for a Father who does not have the Church for a Mother.' He spelt this out in his unflinching loyalty to the Magisterium in the years that followed the Second Vatican Council, and he passed on his rock-like faith and adherence to the Church's teaching to many thousands of souls. The ecumenical spirit which he always practised, flowing as it did from the universal nature of Opus Dei, was demonstrated when the Holy See agreed to his request, as early as 1950, to allow non-Catholics to be appointed as co-operators of Opus Dei.

In 1993 Pope John Paul II paid tribute to 'the spirit of service to the Church that always inspired the life of the founder.'[72] It was a spirit of service that led him to write (in 1936), 'if Opus Dei doesn't serve the Church it serves no purpose at all', and it also led him to take on tasks for the Holy See wherever asked. Such was the case with the territorial prelature of Yauyos, high in the Peruvian Andes, which was entrusted to the pastoral care of Opus Dei in 1958. When a small group of priests of Opus Dei began to work there, there were some places where a priest had not been seen for ninety years.

Freedom

While Catholics are united on the magisterial teaching of dogmas and doctrines, they enjoy the freedom to hold their own opinions on other matters. It follows, therefore, that - within the bounds of the doctrine of the Church - the members are free to act as they wish in their work and their other pursuits, for which they alone are responsible and on which Opus Dei has nothing to say to them.

The founder wrote: 'There are no dogmas in temporal affairs. To try to set up absolute truths in matters where the individual sees things from his own point of view, in terms of his own interest, his cultural preference and his own experience: this insults the dignity of man.' He continued, 'I am of the opinion that a Christian has to be passionately interested in civil and social progress while realising the limitations of his own opinions thus respecting the opinions of others and showing love for legitimate pluralism.'[73] Consequently, as he stated on another occasion, 'In Opus Dei pluralism is desired and loved, not simply tolerated, and in no way is it hindered. Spiritual unity is compatible with variety in temporal matters... Above all when people live up to the faith and realise that men are united not so much by links of sympathy and mutual interest, but above all by the action of the one Spirit.'[74]

Living a vocation to Opus Dei

It is of course impossible to give an example of how a 'typical' member of Opus Dei will live their vocation: each one lives according to the spirit of Opus Dei within their own personal and family circumstances. At the same time there are some common features, because the spirit is the same whether the person concerned is young or old, single or married, a manual worker or an intellectual.

How would a vocation to Opus Dei affect a housewife and mother of a family? Naturally, the daily routine of getting the children up and ready for school and helping them with their problems and their homework when they get home again, the cleaning, the washing, the shopping, the cooking and the thousand and one small tasks of the day will all be there as before: but rather than seeing them as so many chores to be got through she will try to see them as what they really are, the raw material of her holiness.

And in order to sanctify these small daily activities, a housewife - like anyone else - has to be a 'contemplative in the midst of the world,' as Fr Josemaría put it. She will try to find time for weekday Mass on a regular basis. She will make sure she sets aside some time every day for a period of mental prayer, in which the concerns of her day and of her husband and family can be brought to Our Lord. While she is going about her housework she will try to offer that work to God, and because you can't offer God second-rate things she will try to do the work as well as she can within the time constraints. To carry on a conversation with Our Lady - who after all was a housewife and mother too, and therefore knows what it's like - while you are doing the dusting is perfectly possible. In the same way, it is not hard to say aspirations - short prayers from the heart - while you are baking for the school fête.

Naturally, her first apostolate is with her family and especially with her children, encouraging them to take their Christian life seriously, to learn about their faith and to learn how to put it into practice, to teach them to pray. And if she is to teach them she will feel the need to know her own faith better, so she will spend a few minutes every day doing some spiritual reading from the New Testament and from some other book recommended to her in the spiritual guidance she receives. But almost more important is the effort to help the children to pick up good habits, the virtues that are so important for a Christian life. Any mother knows that children need to learn how to be loyal to their friends, and truthful, and cheerful, and generous, to work hard and consistently, to be tidy, and much more besides. And she also knows that these are not virtues that can be picked up overnight: they require a great deal of patience and perseverance on her part. But there are also other opportunities for her to bring Christ to those around her: with other mothers, while she is chatting with them as they wait to pick up their children from school, or helping to run the local playgroup. Or it could be with the shop assistants she meets every day at the local supermarket or with the leaders of the youth club, or football club, or other activities her children go to. Then there are the teachers at school, the parents of her children's friends, and so forth. She does not need to do anything out of the ordinary: the opportunities are there naturally.

In the same way, a member of Opus Dei who is a family man and works as an accountant will continue his daily routine, but will probably start getting up earlier to go to weekday Mass. He will try to make better use of his time at work so as to get home earlier and spend more time with his wife and children, and give more attention to the way his children are growing up. In the office he will try to put into practice the Christian and human virtues, particularly the ones especially relevant to his own work - sound judgement and honesty, good humour when dealing with particularly difficult clients, justice and fairness, concern for others and so on. And like the housewife he will try to further the message of holiness and the need for Christian formation among his friends and colleagues at work. He too will be putting aside some time each day for mental prayer to nourish his spiritual

life, and spiritual reading to help his prayer and his knowledge of his faith. At work he may have a discreet crucifix or
picture of Our Lady on his desk, or possibly as an image on
his computer screen, to help him remember often during his
work that he is in the presence of God. It will also encourage
him to offer up that piece of work for a friend - possibly
someone he wants to talk to in the coffee-break about
prayer, in between asking him how his children got on in the
school play and whether he managed to sort out that client's
tax affairs. At lunchtime he might slip out of the office for a
brief visit to Our Lord in the tabernacle of the local Catholic
church, or to say the Rosary.

Naturally, both the housewife and the accountant will
suggest to some of their friends that they might like to come
with them to retreats or evenings of recollection organised
in their local centre of Opus Dei, or to get spiritual guidance
from the chaplain of the centre. Having seen how much
they get from these activities themselves, they will want
others to benefit from them as well. Of those who attend the
activities on offer in the centres, perhaps very few will join
Opus Dei themselves, but many find there a support for
their spiritual lives and an impetus to help them to be apostles among their own friends and acquaintances.

Among the members of Opus Dei who have died, several
have had their cause of beatification started. The earliest,
Isidoro Zorzano, was born in Buenos Aires, and worked as a
railway engineer until his death in 1943. His hidden and

silent dedication was one of the foundations on which Fr Josemaría was able to rely to build Opus Dei in the early years. A second, Montserrat Grases, was a young student in Barcelona who died of cancer in 1959 at only seventeen years of age. She was known for her cheerfulness and the serenity with which she accepted her final illness.

Others who have died with a reputation for holiness are also attracting private devotion. One, Eduardo Ortiz, was a doctor and Professor of Pathology at various Spanish universities before joining the newly founded faculty of medicine in the University of Navarre at Pamplona. He was married with seven children and was known for his exceptionally hard work and kindness to his patients. It was said that his day began very early and usually ended very early the next morning. He died in 1985. Another, Toni Zweifel, was a Swiss engineer at the Institute for Thermodynamics in Zürich. He helped to found a charity supporting projects worldwide for the promotion of women and the family, and was its director until his death from leukemia in 1989. He was known as a person with a great sense of humour at the same time as being a scientist of great competence. A third, Ernesto Cofiño, was a Guatemalan paediatrician and professor, with five children of his own, who studied in the University of Paris. He spent much of his retirement working for organisations dedicated to furthering the education and training of peasants and workers living in deprived circumstances, before his death in 1991 at the age of 92.

OPUS DEI IN THE CHURCH

What is a personal prelature?

The concept of a personal prelature was suggested by the Second Vatican Council and then established by Paul VI in 1966.[75] It was proposed as an answer to the search for more flexible structures to deal with the needs of the contemporary apostolate. The Council Fathers suggested that, among other institutions, 'special dioceses, or personal prelatures' could be established 'to carry out special pastoral tasks for the benefit of different social groups in different regions or among any race in any part of the world.'[76]

A personal prelature is part of the jurisdictional/hierarchical structure of the Church. Most jurisdictions in the Church are territorial, as in the case of a diocese, where the faithful who belong to it are determined according to their territory or domicile. However, jurisdiction is not always linked to territory, but may depend on other criteria, such as employment, religious rite, immigrant status, or agreement with the jurisdictional body in question. The last-mentioned applies in the case of military ordinariates (military bishoprics) and personal prelatures.

Personal prelatures, as envisaged by the Second Vatican Council, are made up of a pastor, a presbyterate (clergy) consisting of secular priests, and men and women lay faithful. The prelate, who may be a bishop, is appointed by the Pope, and governs the prelature with power of governance and jurisdiction.

The Church has established personal prelatures within its hierarchical structure, with the special feature that the faithful of the prelature continue to belong to their local church and to the diocese where they live.

For these and other reasons, personal prelatures are clearly different from religious institutes and the consecrated life in general, as well as from associations and movements of the faithful.

The Code of Canon Law outlines the purposes of personal prelatures and the way they are governed, noting that one of their main purposes is to carry out special pastoral enterprises or apostolic tasks.[77] Each personal prelature is regulated by general Church law and by its own statutes approved by the Holy See.

Opus Dei as a personal prelature

In order to understand why the structure of a personal prelature is the most suited to the foundational charism of Opus Dei, we first of all have to appreciate the problem that Fr Josemaría faced. In 1928 there was no provision in Church law for an institution that was international in character and that consisted of secular priests and laity - men and women, celibate and married - dedicating themselves completely to sanctity and apostolate in and through their everyday duties and responsibilities. There was the further complication that Canon Law did not allow the possibility of priests being incardinated into such an institution. (All priests must come under the authority of a bishop or some other cleric who has the authority to govern within the Church: this is called incardination. Priests other than those belonging to a religious order are normally incardinated in a diocese.) Fr Josemaría, therefore, had to find a formula that would safeguard the secular and international character of Opus Dei as well as its unity of priests and lay people. It was a task that was to last beyond his own lifetime, but which ended with the solution that he had mapped out.

Pope John Paul II set up Opus Dei as a personal prelature in 1982, after years of study and after hearing the views of bishops throughout the world, wherever Opus Dei was already established. The step was something that had been foreseen, as the constitution setting up Opus Dei as a prelature suggests: 'From the time when the Second Vatican Ecumenical Council introduced into the legislation of the Church... the figure of the personal prelatures, to carry out specific pastoral activities, it was seen clearly that this juridical figure was perfectly suited to Opus Dei.'

The 'special pastoral task' of Opus Dei is to proclaim the universal calling to holiness and to the apostolate in the midst of the world. This mission, then, is as wide as the whole Church and is open to all the baptised who live in the world. People sometimes ask: If the teaching applies to everyone, and if it consists in sanctifying the ordinary duties of each day, then why do you need a special institution for it? The answer is that the institution of Opus Dei exists to spread this message by putting it into concrete form in individuals and families the length and breadth of the world. In the words of the founder, Opus Dei is 'a small part of the Church', but at the service of the whole Church.[78] Like the Church herself, then, Opus Dei has both an invisible and visible element to it - it participates in the message of the Church and in its visible structure.

The Opus Dei prelature is a body that belongs to the pastoral and structural organisation of the Church, and its prelate is a member of the hierarchy of the Church. Like dioceses, territorial prelatures and military ordinariates, it has its own proper autonomy and ordinary jurisdiction. For that reason, it depends directly on the Pope through the Congregation for Bishops. Like a military ordinariate its jurisdiction is personal rather than territorial: it extends to those people who put themselves under the prelate by joining Opus Dei because they understand that to be their specific Christian path.

Members of Opus Dei join by means of a contract - a 'commitment of love', the founder called it - which covers the areas of their spiritual life and their ascetical, doctrinal and apostolic formation. These are matters of freedom for lay people, who can choose for themselves what type of spirituality to follow. As a result, the authority of the prelate does not overlap with that of the diocesan bishop: they are exercised in different areas. The lay faithful of Opus Dei continue to be faithful of the diocese where they live and they remain under the authority of the local bishop in exactly the same matters as all the other baptised faithful.

The statutes of Opus Dei lay down procedures for the harmonious co-ordination between the prelature and the dioceses in which it operates. The regional authorities of the prelature maintain the necessary personal contact with the diocesan bishop informing him of the apostolic work of the prelature. The prelature never begins apostolic work or opens any centres without the previous knowledge and agreement of the local bishop. The regional authorities of Opus Dei try to foster unity with the bishops, and encourage members to read and put into practice the guidelines of their local bishop and the bishops' conference. The apostolate of the faithful of Opus Dei should, with the grace of God, be reflected in the parishes where they live and work: in conversions, increased attendance at Mass and the reception of the sacraments, the spreading of the Gospel to those separated from the faith. Members try to help those in need and are always willing to co-operate in catechesis in the parish and in any other activities connected with the parish or the diocese, as far as is compatible with their own work and family duties.

Incorporation into the prelature

The contract members make with the prelature is an official declaration in the presence of witnesses, which establishes mutual commitments. The aspiring members put themselves under the jurisdiction of the prelate as far as their spiritual life and personal apostolate is concerned. The prelature, for its part, commits itself to provide the spiritual, formational (educational) and pastoral care of the individual members. The formation Opus Dei gives is aimed above all at deepening their spiritual life. For each one this involves prayer, mortification and the reception of the sacraments, and also improving their knowledge of their faith through studying the doctrinal and moral teaching of the Church.

In order to achieve this, members attend short weekly classes on doctrinal and ascetical matters and also receive spiritual direction on a regular basis. Once a month they set aside a few hours for quiet recollection, which includes meditations directed by a priest of the prelature, talks, time for private prayer, and some liturgical act, often benediction. Each year they attend a retreat lasting several days, and also a course or workshop in which they study the teaching of the Church and other subjects to help their spiritual lives and their apostolate. Similar means are also offered to co-operators, to the young people who participate in the activities offered in the centres, and to other people who may want to make use of them.

The priests are ordained from among the laymen of the prelature and come from both the numeraries and associates. The prelate invites them to the priesthood, but they are free to remain laymen if they prefer. They are ordained to serve all souls, and attend principally to the faithful of the prelature and its specific apostolates. They depend completely on the prelate who is responsible for their pastoral appointments and for their sustenance. At the same time they maintain friendly and fraternal relations with their diocesan colleagues and may form part of the senate or pastoral council of priests. With the consent of the prelate they may be appointed to positions in the diocese, as parish clergy or helping in the curial offices.

Joining Opus Dei takes place as follows. First, the applicant requests admission in writing. Admission is granted after a minimum waiting period of six months from the date of their letter of application. After a further period of a year the candidate can be incorporated into the prelature by means of the contract mentioned above, which must be renewed annually on 19th March, the feast of St Joseph. A minimum of five years after making their first contract (and thus six and a half years after their first application) the member may make his or her incorporation definitive. The minimum age for this is twenty-three.

The Priestly Society of the Holy Cross

The Priestly Society of the Holy Cross is an association of clergy which is intrinsically united to Opus Dei. It is made up both of priests of the prelature (who have come from its lay faithful) and diocesan priests who wish to belong to the society, responding to a divine vocation which leads them to seek sanctity according to the spirit of Opus Dei by means of the exercise of their priestly ministry. Diocesan priests who join the society remain incardinated in their own dioceses and dependent on their own bishop. The prelate of Opus Dei is the president of the Society of the Holy Cross, which simply has the organisational structure that is normal for associations with exclusively spiritual ends. As president he has no jurisdiction over the diocesan priests who join - jurisdiction remains with their local bishop.

The spiritual support which the association offers is aimed at encouraging the perfect fulfilment of priestly duties, as well as fostering the union of each priest with his own bishop and a fraternal spirit among his fellow-priests. The spiritual and formative activities of members of the Priestly Society are co-ordinated to ensure that they do not interfere in any way with the pastoral work entrusted to them by the bishop. At the present about two thousand diocesan clergy belong to the Priestly Society of the Holy Cross world-wide.

The co-operators of Opus Dei

The co-operators of Opus Dei are men and women who support the apostolate of the prelature with their prayers (if they are believers), their work and their almsgiving. They are not members of Opus Dei. They may benefit from the graces and indulgences conceded by the Church to those who help with the work of Opus Dei, and they benefit from the prayers of the faithful of the prelature on their behalf. If they wish, they may also participate in the means of formation that the prelature offers. Opus Dei counts among its co-operators not only Catholics, but also men and women of other Christian denominations and of other religions, together with numerous non-believers. What they share is a common desire to participate and collaborate in various initiatives of the prelature.

How Opus Dei is organised

A characteristic of the way Opus Dei is governed is its collegial character. The prelate resides in Rome and governs with the co-operation of councils made up mainly of lay people, one for the apostolates carried out by men and another, similar though independent, for the women's apostolates. The prelate is chosen by an assembly of electors. His election must be confirmed by the Pope, who thereby confers the office of prelate on the person elected. The appointment is held for life. The present prelate, who is the second successor of Fr Josemaría, is Bishop Javier Echevarría, who had previously been vicar general of the prelature and before that an aide and close collaborator of Fr Josemaría. He was appointed in 1994, and consecrated a bishop by the Pope in 1995.

At the next level, the prelature is divided into territorial divisions called regions, which normally, though not always, coincide with the area of a country. At the head of each region is a regional vicar who, like the prelate, has his councils, one for the men's apostolates and another independent one for the women's apostolates. The regional vicar in Great Britain since July 1998 is Mgr Nicholas Morrish.

At the local level are to be found the centres of Opus Dei, whose task is to organise the means of formation and pastoral care of the faithful of the prelature in their area. Each centre is directed by a 'local council' or committee made up of a director and at least two other lay people. In addition, a chaplain is designated for the priestly attention of each centre.

Financial matters

The faithful of the prelature earn their living with their work and are expected to be financially self-sufficient, providing for themselves and their families. In addition to covering their own expenses they also endeavour to contribute to the pastoral needs of the prelature. These include the costs of maintaining and training the priests of the prelature, the running of the offices of the prelature at central and regional level, and almsgiving. Furthermore, financial support is given to parents and near relatives of the numeraries and associates in the event of serious financial hardship.

Many co-operators of Opus Dei also assist the activities and initiatives throughout the world by their almsgiving. The apostolic initiatives of the Opus Dei prelature are owned and run by charities or other bodies that are set up by members of the prelature and other people, with Opus Dei providing the spiritual direction: for this reason, the founder would say that Opus Dei as such owns nothing. These apostolic initiatives are financed by the work of members, co-operators, and many friends and benefactors throughout the world who appreciate the good that they are doing both humanly and spiritually.

APOSTOLIC INITIATIVES

'Opus Dei's main activity consists in offering its faithful, and other people, the spiritual means they need in order to live as good Christians in the midst of the world', Fr Josemaría explained. 'It helps them to learn Christ's doctrine and the Church's teachings,' so that they can then carry out a work of personal apostolate with those around them. This personal apostolate is the principal apostolic activity of Opus Dei. The founder went on to say, 'However, moved by a desire to contribute to the solution of each society's problems, which are closely related to the Christian ideal, it also has some other corporate activities. Our criterion in this field is that Opus Dei, whose aims are exclusively spiritual, can only carry out corporately activities that clearly constitute an immediate Christian service, an apostolate. It would be ridiculous to think that Opus Dei as such could mine coal or run any type of commercial venture.'[79]

Consequently, the apostolic initiatives promoted by members of Opus Dei, in collaboration with others, are usually of an educational, social or medical nature, such as schools, universities and university residences, inner-city projects, dispensaries and rural promotion centres in poorer countries. These are always civil entities,[80] and the responsibility for them is assumed by the individuals who have set them up and not by Opus Dei. Each initiative is financed in the same way as any venture of a similar type: by fees, grants and donations. They often run at a deficit and therefore rely on subsidies from public authorities, donations from grant making bodies or from private individuals, especially members of Opus Dei and co-operators.

The prelature can assume responsibility for ensuring the Christian spirit of such an undertaking by providing doctrinal guidance and pastoral care. A formal agreement to this effect is established with those in charge, in accordance with the statutes of the undertaking. All ventures of this kind fully respect the freedom of individual consciences and are open to people of all creeds, races and social conditions.

The Opus Dei prelature can enter into various types of agreements with apostolic activities. In the case of the 'corporate works' of apostolate, Opus Dei morally guarantees the Christian orientation of the activities they provide. In other cases, Opus Dei provides spiritual help, but without officially giving any moral guarantee as regards the formation offered. This spiritual assistance can take a variety of forms, such as priestly ministry or religion classes.

Such agreements with the prelature do not modify the civil nature of these activities in any way. Responsibility for their functioning and government always rests with their directors and not with the Opus Dei prelature.

Opus Dei's first corporate work of apostolate in Great Britain, in 1952, was Netherhall House, an inter-collegiate university residence for men in Hampstead, London. A larger purpose-built extension funded in part by the British Council and the Greater London Council was opened by the Queen Mother in 1966. The final phase was inaugurated by the Duchess of Kent in 1995, increasing the capacity to about 100 students. Netherhall House admits students of all faiths and none.

Other student residences in Britain include Ashwell House (also in London), Greygarth Hall and Coniston Hall (both in Manchester). There are also two smaller centres in Oxford that organise activities for students: Grandpont House and Winton.

Courses of various types for the general public, including preached retreats, are organised regularly in two conference centres: Wickenden Manor (near East Grinstead, West Sussex) and Thornycroft Hall (near Macclesfield, Cheshire).

Catering education centres such as Lakefield, in London, offer NVQ (National Vocational Qualification) courses for school leavers wishing to gain qualifications for the hospitality industry.

As well as the on-going adult Christian formation provided, Opus Dei centres organise courses and seminars on spiritual, moral, educational and cultural themes. A number run activities for young people, examples being Kelston Club (Wandsworth) and Tamezin Club (Chelsea), both in London, and Dunreath Club in Glasgow.

Abroad, corporate works of Opus Dei include schools, such as Strathmore and Kianda in Kenya, and educational initiatives at tertiary level, such as the University of Piura in Peru, and the University of Asia and the Pacific in the Philippines. The University of Navarre, in Pamplona, Spain, has twenty departments and includes a university hospital. Other undertakings include the Lagos Business School in Nigeria, the IESE Business School in Barcelona, and a hospital and bio-medical centre in Rome.

Social projects

Among the corporate works are many social projects. In his memoirs Fr Pedro Casciaro, the first member of Opus Dei to go to Latin America and for many years regional vicar in Mexico, tells a moving story which occurred on one of his journeys to the interior. 'I was waiting in the car at a petrol station when an indigenous Indian of about fourteen years of age came up to the window and said to me. "Father, take me with you." "Where do you want me to take you?" I asked. The answer came back, "Anywhere; I want to serve God."'[81]

This episode led to deep thought being given to the development of centres of education for the rural population in Mexico. A year later a ranch that had been destroyed by fire during the Mexican revolution at the beginning of the twentieth century and left empty was donated. After decades of work this site at Montefalco houses four schools for the rural population in the area:

a school of home economics, an agricultural school, a women's institute and a teachers' training college. This initiative has given rise to many others and there have sprung up medical centres and dispensaries and vocational schools in underdeveloped areas throughout Latin America.

Similar social projects exist in other parts of the world. Punlaan, in Manila, is a specialist professional school for the catering and tourist industry, as is the Lycée Professionnel Kimbondo in Kinshasa. The Monkole Medical Centre, in the same city, serves over 30,000 patients. Attached to Monkole is the Higher Institute of Nursing, which prepares young Congolese women for the nursing profession.

The ELIS centre in Rome, which was opened by Pope Paul VI in 1965, was set up to train and educate the children of poor migrant workers who had settled in that part of the city. The project was entrusted to Opus Dei by Pope John XXIII and the name ELIS stands for *Educazione, Lavoro, Istruzione, Sport* (Education, Work, Instruction, Sport). It is financed by the local authority of Lazio and the Italian Foreign Ministry and now includes programmes for students from less developed countries such as Albania and Somalia. A similar project to ELIS is Tajamar in Madrid, which originally catered for migrant workers from the south of Spain.

Midtown Sports and Cultural Center and Metro Achievement Center are inner-city projects in Chicago. Situated in multiracial neighbourhoods, they both offer sports and programmes of academic and spiritual formation. The education is aimed at equipping young people from disadvantaged backgrounds to achieve a better start in life. Of Midtown's students, 95% finish high school and 60% go on to college, more than double the averages of their peers.

In addition to the apostolic initiatives for which Opus Dei takes responsibility or provides spiritual help, there are also of course many other ventures which are set up by the personal initiative of individual members of Opus Dei and others.

SOME FINAL THOUGHTS

Opus Dei and the Second Vatican Council

The Second Vatican Council condemned as 'one of the gravest errors of our time... the dichotomy between the faith which many profess and the practice of their daily lives.'[82] As Christians we are always exposed to the danger of falling into one of two extremes: either we can let the present world and its achievements, anxieties and luxuries take on excessive importance and put our religion aside, or equally falsely, we can consider the present life as irrelevant because of the overriding importance of getting to Heaven. This apparent dilemma was expressed by a teacher in a Catholic school some years ago who remarked to a friend, 'On the one hand we are telling the children they have to work hard so they can get on in the world. On the other, we're saying none of this is what really matters.' This view does not take account of the continuity between human life and supernatural life, sometimes expressed in the phrase, 'unity of life.'

Fr Josemaría emphasised that the supernatural is in harmony with the natural order, and that grace perfects nature and does not destroy it. Supernatural virtues are built on the human virtues and the kingdom of Heaven is attained by fulfilling both the duties of one's faith

and one's everyday obligations. For a Catholic, therefore, there is a unity between the spiritual, family,
work-related and social aspects of our life. 'There is a
type of secularist outlook that one comes across, and
also another approach which one might call "pietistic",
both of which share the view that Christians are not
fully and entirely human. According to the former, the
demands of the Gospel are such as to stifle our human
qualities; whereas for the latter, human nature is so
fallen that it threatens and undermines the purity of the
faith. The result either way is the same. They both fail
to grasp the full significance of Christ's Incarnation,
they do not see that "the Word was made flesh".'[83] So
for the school pupils mentioned in the previous paragraph,
hard work really *does* matter. It is not just a vehicle for
getting on in life: it can and should be a means for
their sanctification.

Pope John Paul II said to a group of Opus Dei members in 1979: 'Your institution has as its objective the
sanctification of ordinary life while remaining in the
world, in one's own sphere of work, and in one's profession: to live the gospel in the world, living immersed in
the world, but to transform it and redeem it through the
love of Christ himself. Yours is truly a high ideal, for
from the beginning it anticipated the theology of the laity
which was to be a characteristic of the church of the
Council and after the Council.'[84]

John Paul II embraces Bishop Alvaro del Portillo after the beatification of the Founder of Opus Dei (18th May 1992).

The re-evangelisation of society

The vision of Fr Josemaría was to contribute to opening 'the divine paths of the earth',[85] showing that all honest human activities are ways to reach God. In proposing to 'place Jesus Christ at the summit of all human activities,'[86] the founder of Opus Dei put forward the same theme that Pope John Paul II has proclaimed over and over again since the very beginning of his pontificate, and has repeated once more in his letter for the new millennium: the re-Christianisation of modern society. We might ask if it is possible to change the secularised world in which we live: the answer to this was given to Fr Josemaría in the City of London in 1958. Walking among the great financial buildings of the Square Mile, he was overwhelmed momentarily by the display of earthly power and wealth and at the same time by the lack of faith that seemed to be all around him. As he wondered if all of this could be given back to God, he clearly heard Our Lord saying inside him, 'You can't, but I can.'

The growth of Opus Dei and the way it has spread around the world can only be attributed to the fact that it is a divine and not a human undertaking, with a message relevant for our times. Pope Paul VI described Opus Dei as a 'living expression of the perennial youthfulness of the Church.' In answer to a journalist's question about whether Opus Dei could sustain the enthusiasm of the early years, Fr Josemaría said, 'The Work is based not on enthusiasm but on faith.'[87] And Pope John Paul II urged the faithful of Opus Dei gathered in Rome for the beatification of the founder in 1992 to 'be fully committed to the cause of evangelisation through your faithful witness to the Church's faith and doctrine in the vast world of human affairs and through your generous participation in the Church's mission. As a leaven in society, bring your talents to bear in public and private life at every level, proclaiming in word and deed the truth about man's transcendent dignity. Following the teaching of your founder, respond generously to the universal call to the fullness of the Christian life and the perfection of charity, thus laying the foundation for a more human way of life and a more just and equitable society.'[88]

If you would like further information about any aspect of the Opus Dei prelature, please contact the Opus Dei Information Office at

5 Orme Court,
London W2 4RL,
Tel: 020-7221 9176,
e-mail london@opusdei.org
web site *http://www.opusdei.org*

BIBLIOGRAPHY

Josemaría Escrivá,
The Way (1939)
Conversations with Mgr Escrivá (1968)
Christ is Passing By (1973)
Friends of God (1977)
Way of the Cross (1981)
In Love with the Church (1986)
Furrow (1986)
The Forge (1987)

About Opus Dei

Giuseppe Romano, *Opus Dei: Who? How? Why?*
(New York 1994)
Vittorio Messori, *Opus Dei* (New York 1997)

About the Founder

Peter Berglar, *Opus Dei: Life and Work of its Founder*
(Princeton 1993)
Alvaro del Portillo, *Immersed in God* (Princeton 1996)
Andres Vásquez de Prada, *The Founder of Opus Dei*,
vol. I (Princeton 2001)
Ethel Tolansky & Helena Scott (CTS booklet),
Josemaria Escriva (London 2001)

Endnotes

1. Throughout this booklet references are made to the 'faithful of the prelature', just as in speaking of a diocese one may refer to the faithful of that diocese or to the Catholic faithful in general.

2. *Novo millennio ineunte*, 29.

3. *L'Osservatore Romano*, 18th March 2001.

4. *Christ is Passing By*, 105.

5. Matthew 5:48.

6. Cf. *Christ is Passing By*, 132.

7. *Lumen Gentium*, 40.

8. *Lumen Gentium*, 31.

9. *Apostolicam Actuositatem*, 5.

10. *Ephesians* 1:4.

11. Cf. *Christ is Passing By*, 46.

12. *Conversations with Monsignor Escrivá*, 114.

13. *Ibid*, 114.

14. *Ibid*, 113.

15. *Letter to Diognetus*, 6.

16. *Lumen Gentium*, 31.

17. Mark 7:37

18. Cf. *Friends of God*, 61.

19. *Apostolicam Actuositatem*, 2.

20. Cf. Luke 19:13.

21. *Apostolicam Actuositatem*, 7.

22. *Ibid*, 7.

23. *Instruction on the Laity*, foreword.

24. Colossians 1:19-20.

25. *Christ is Passing By*, 112.

26. *The Way*, 335.

27. Cf. *Friends of God*, 308.

28. Genesis 2:15

29. *The Forge*, 702.

30. *L'Osservatore Romano*, 18th/19th May 1992.

31. *Lumen Gentium*, 41.

32. *Conversations*, 91.

33. *Catechism of the Catholic Church*, 1546.

34. See *Instruction on the Laity*, section '*Theological Principles*', 1.

35 *Christifideles Laici*, 1-2. Cf. Matthew 20:1-16.

36 Matthew 5:13-15.

37 *Conversations*, 116.

38 John 12:32 (Vulgate).

39 *The Way*, 301.

40 *Ibid*, 790.

41 *The Way*, 799.

42 1 Samuel 3:9.

43 Cf. Luke 14:16-20.

44 Cf. Matthew 19:29.

45 Matthew 8:22.

46 Luke 9:59-62.

47 *Conversations*, 104.

48 Article in *Il Gazzetino*, Venice, 25th July 1978, translated in *The Universe*, London, 29th September 1978, with the title 'Go to work on a smile!'

49 See *Veritatis Splendor*, Chapter 1

50 Isaiah 1:17.

51 *Christ is Passing By*, 184.

52 *The Way*, 463.

53 Article 'The riches of the Faith', in *ABC*, Madrid, 2nd November 1969.

54 2 Peter 1:4.

55 *Christ is Passing By*, 103.

56 *Christ is Passing By*, 64.

57 Romans 8:28.

58 Cf. John 14:27, 16:22.

59 *The Way*, 309, 310.

60 *Christ is Passing By*, 58.

61 *Christ is Passing By*, 75.

62 *The Way*, 81.

63 *Friends of God*, 299.

64 *Friends of God*, 244.

65 *Christ is Passing By*, Foreword (among others).

66 Cf. Luke 9:23.

67 *The Way*, 205.

68 I Corinthians 9:25, 27.

69 *Lumen Gentium*, 62.

70 *The Way*, 495.

71 *Friends of God*, 293.

72 *L'Osservatore Romano*, 27th October 1993.

[73] Article 'The riches of the Faith', in *ABC*, Madrid, 2nd November 1969.

[74] *Conversations*, 67.

[75] The term first appears in in *Presbyterorum Ordinis*; they were established by the motu proprio *Ecclesiae Sanctae*.

[76] *Presbyterorum Ordinis*, 10.

[77] Canons 294-97.

[78] Rodríguez et al, Opus Dei in the Church, p. 1.

[79] *Conversations*, 27.

[80] These apostolic initiatives are separate from the institutions of an ecclesiastical nature entrusted to or promoted by the prelature itself, e.g. the Pontifical University of the Holy Cross in Rome.

[81] Pedro Casciaro, *Dream and your dreams will fall short* (London 1997), p. 329.

[82] *Gaudium et Spes*, 43.

[83] *Friends of God*, 74.

[84] *L'Osservatore Romano*, 27th August 1979.

[85] *The Forge*, 553.

[86] *Ibid*, 685.

[87] *Conversations*, 68.

[88] *L'Osservatore Romano*, 22nd May 1992.

CTS
MEMBERSHIP

We hope you have enjoyed reading this booklet. If you would like to read more of our booklets or find out more about CTS - why not do one of the following?

1. Join our Readers CLUB.
We will send you a copy of every new booklet we publish, through the post to your address. You'll get 20% off the price too.

2. Support our work and Mission.
Become a CTS Member. Every penny you give will help spread the faith throughout the world. What's more, you'll be entitled to special offers exclusive to CTS Members.

3. Ask for our Information Pack.
Become part of the CTS Parish Network by selling CTS publications in your own parish.

**Call us now on 020 7640 0042 or return this form to us at CTS, 40-46 Harleyford Road, London SE11 5AY
Fax: 020 7640 0046 email: info@cts-online.org.uk**

❏ I would like to join the *CTS Readers Club*

❏ Please send me details of how to join CTS as a *Member*

❏ Please send me a *CTS Information Pack*

Name:...

Address:...

....

Post Code:...

Phone:..

email address:...

Registered charity no. 218951.
Registered in England as a company limited by guarantee no.57374.